{ CITIESCAPE }

KATHMANDU*

{ CITIESCAPE }

JOE BINDLOSS

CONTENTS*

VITAL STATS*

NAME Kathmandu **AKA** City of Temples
DATE OF BIRTH AD 723 **HEIGHT** 1355m
SIZE 600 sq km (Kathmandu Valley)
ADDRESS Nepal **POPULATION** 1.1 million

PEOPLE*

{ *THE POPULATION OF KATHMANDU IS FAIRLY MODEST, BUT EVERYONE IS SQUEEZED INTO A TINY AREA** by the steep walls of the Kathmandu Valley. As a result, Kathmandu has grown upwards rather than outwards. High-rises are appearing all over the valley and 2739 people are squeezed into every square kilometre, compared to just four people per square kilometre in the high plains of the Himalaya. Things aren't likely to get much better, either – the average Kathmandu family has four children and the population is set to double over the next 20 years. }

DESPITE CREEPING MODERNISATION, Kathmandu residents are deeply traditional and people are still defined by their marital status – married women wear a red tilak mark on their foreheads and widows are forbidden from wearing red, the most popular colour in the valley. Religion plays a huge part in the day-to-day life of most residents – 85% are Hindu, 10% are Buddhist and 3% are Muslim.

9.

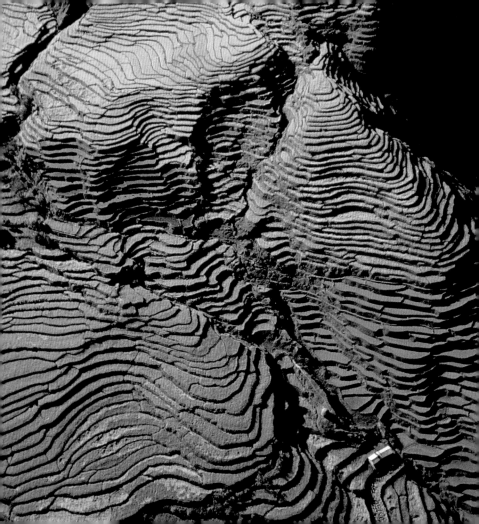

ANATOMY*

{ }

* KATHMANDU SPRAWLS ACROSS THE BOTTOM OF A BOWL-SHAPED MOUNTAIN VALLEY, SHADED BY THE TOWERING PEAKS OF THE GANESH HIMALAYA. The official centre of town is the Royal Palace, but most of the famous temples and monuments are clustered around Durbar Marg at the south end of town. Between the two are the winding, brick-lined bazaars of Asan Tole and Chhetrapati, and Thamel, the main traveller hang-out. No part of Kathmandu is completely 'new', but the shopping centres and airline offices are concentrated around New Road and Durbar Marg. Most people get around by taxi or rickshaw or just walk – the backstreets are full of hidden temples and atmospheric courtyards.

KATHMANDU SHARES the valley with the equally historic cities of Patan and Bhaktapur but it's hard to tell where one stops and the other begins. Patan is just south of Kathmandu on the south bank of the Bagmati River, while Bhaktapur is east on the far side of the airport.

PERSON ALITY*

{ ***IT IS HARD TO FIND WORDS THAT DO JUSTICE TO WONDERFUL KATHMANDU.** }
One ridge away from the highest mountains in the world, and thronged by a million Hindus and Buddhists, this princely city is the archetypal mountain kingdom – mystical, magical and arcane. Temples loom out of the mist around every corner and the cobbled streets resound with the chanting of mantras and the chiming of temple bells. At dusk, the city is transformed into a cut-out of stupas, prayer flags and temple spires. On clear days, a wall of snow-covered mountains rises behind Kathmandu and eagles soar majestically overhead on the high Tibetan winds – it's like the special effects from *The Lord of the Rings*, but right there, alive, in the real world.

THE MAIN REASON for Kathmandu's remarkable state of preservation is its unique geographical situation. There are only two roads out of the Kathmandu Valley, one going north to Lhasa in Tibet and the other winding down to the Terai plains – a five-hour journey to cover a distance of 50 kilometres. Historically, this was Kathmandu's

13.

best defence against foreign invaders. Unlike India and Tibet, Nepal was never conquered by the British.

THE CITY'S METEORIC rise to fame began in 1769 when the Gurkha king Prithvi Narayan Shah swept eastwards from his base at Gorkha, conquering the towns on the valley rim and isolating Kathmandu, Bhaktapur and Patan from the outside world. This marked the start of the golden age of Kathmandu architecture – temple-strewn Durbar Square has barely changed since. As the city grew, the natural fortifications of the valley walls became a hindrance rather than an asset. Everything had to be trekked in from the plains of India and builders had nowhere to go but up, explaining the rather chaotic skyline of leaning brick towers.

POLITICS ALSO PLAYED a role in Kathmandu's state of suspended animation. From 1816 to 1950, Nepal was completely cut off from the outside world, vanishing into legend as another forbidden kingdom of the Himalaya. The Swiss explorer Toni Hagen was the first European allowed in and he walked all over the country, setting a precedent for the 200,000 trekkers who now visit every year.

KATHMANDU IS TRYING hard to make up for lost time, but many of its day-to-day essentials still arrive via the crowded mountain road from the Indian border. And while broadband Internet and ATM banking have reached the city, there's no reliable mobile phone signal and the network is often turned off completely during times of political crisis, which maintains the sense of isolation. On the other hand, few modern cities can match Kathmandu for history, scenery and culture – the chapters that follow offer glimpses into its spirituality, energy and diversity. Use the silence for meditation and yoga before leaping into the most animated traveller scene in Asia.

SPIRITUAL*

{ * **THERE'S SOMETHING IMPRESSIVE ABOUT A LARGE GROUP OF PEOPLE WHO ALL BELIEVE THE SAME THING.** There are places in Kathmandu that have a spiritual energy you can almost sense in the air, like the buzzing of overhead power lines. The spirituality of Kathmandu seems to resonate with most travellers – not many leave without giving at least a moment's thought to their position in the universe. }

PERHAPS IT HAS something to do with the location, surrounded by the highest peaks in the world. Or maybe it's the clear mountain air, or the hundreds of Hindu temples and Buddhist stupas littered across the Kathmandu Valley. Or perhaps it's just that spirituality seems to make more sense when travelling, away from the material concerns of gas bills and the daily commute. Whether the spiritual feel-good factor survives the transition back to normal life is another matter, but quite a few travellers arrive agnostic and go home wearing the red robes of Buddhist monks.

THE KATHMANDU VALLEY is famous for its multi-tiered pagoda temples. Statues of Hindu deities are housed in small sanctums at the base of the towers and worshippers

17.

pray, individually or in family groups, standing outside the door. Shikhara temples, also common in the city, have a tapering, pyramidal tower representing Mount Meru, the celestial abode of the gods. Buddhist stupas also have a strictly defined structure, symbolising core elements of Buddhist philosophy. Each level of the stupa represents one of the five elements – the base is earth, the dome water, the spire fire, the umbrella air and the pinnacle ether. Many of the temples dotted around the valley are world-famous, including the Buddhist stupa of Swayambhunath, the fabulous Bodhnath stupa and the Hindu temple of Pashupatinath.

IT IS UNIQUELY involving to witness worship at Kathmandu's temples and shrines. Religion infuses all aspects of life for Nepalis and few locals would bat an eyelid at the idea of reincarnation, miracles or gods living right here on earth. Understanding a bit about the Hindu and Buddhist religions will help you understand why many Nepalis wear red rice on their foreheads and why dozens of goats walk into the temples of Kali and Durga but very few walk out. Leather is banned from most Hindu temples out of respect for Nandi, the vehicle of Lord Shiva, and Buddhists only ever walk clockwise around stupas. Spirituality is really let off the leash during Kathmandu's festivals, when people haul huge chariots through the streets and hold boisterous masked parades to drive away demons and celebrate the passing seasons.

CONSIDERING THE IMPORTANCE of spirituality to the locals, it's surprising that their sacred centres are open to all: visitors are welcome at most of the temples and Buddhist stupas and monasteries in the Kathmandu Valley, with the notable exception of Pashupatinath.

FOOD FOR THE GODS*

{ *SHOWING RESPECT FOR THE GODS IS AN ESSENTIAL PART OF DAILY LIFE IN KATHMANDU.** Every morning women walk through the streets carrying a plate, usually copper, filled with an assortment of goodies. They are not delivering breakfast. The food, flowers, water and money will be offered to temple idols as part of the morning puja (prayers). }

EVERY MORNING and evening, thousands of Hindus take time out to offer puja at temples and shrines across the city. Each offering is sprinkled onto the image of the deity in a set order and a bell is rung to let the gods know. The ceremony also involves prayers, meditation and ritual washing.

AT THE END of the ceremony, devotees receive a tilak mark on the forehead and a gift of prasad (blessed food) from the temple priests. Women return home to give a small portion of the blessed food to each member of the household.

21.

BODHNATH*

{ ***IF YOU HAD TO PICK ONE PLACE THAT EXPRESSED THE ENERGY AND ATMO-SPHERE OF KATHMANDU, IT WOULD BE BODHNATH,** the great Buddhist stupa on the eastern side of the Kathmandu Valley. It's the religious centre for Nepal's Tibetan population, one of the few places where their culture is vibrant and unfettered. }

EVERY DAY from before dawn thousands of Buddhist pilgrims complete the ceremonial circumnavigation of the stupa, moving clockwise around the gleaming dome in a continuous human tide, beneath a rainbow-coloured canopy of fluttering prayer flags. Here and there in the crowd you'll see the wind-weathered faces of refugees from the high plains of Tibet, and shaven-headed monks in carmine robes spinning prayer wheels and murmuring the mantra 'Om Mani Padme Hum' (Hail to the Jewel in the Lotus). The most devoted pilgrims measure out the route with their own bodies, laying face down on the ground, then getting up and taking a few steps before dropping back down, in the ultimate act of ritual prostration.

BODHNATH HAS ALWAYS been associated with Tibetan Buddhism. One of the major trade routes from Lhasa went through Sankhu, so Bodhnath lies at the traders' entry to Kathmandu – presumably making it a convenient place to give thanks for a successful journey over the Himalaya.

PROBABLY THE MOST vivid rituals of Tibetan Buddhism are its masked dances, featuring outlandish costumes and gaudy, frightening masks representing animals, monsters and deities. The most animated performances take place during the Tibetan New Year celebrations of Losar in February. Monks don the masks and launch into surreal spinning chaam dances – which tell stories from the founding days of Tibetan Buddhism – accompanied by a chaotic clashing of cymbals, beating of drums and honking of temple horns.

SWAYAMBHUNATH *

{ * **THE BUDDHIST STUPA OF SWAYAMBHUNATH IS REPUTED TO BE THE OLDEST IN NEPAL.** Some sources say it was erected over 2000 years ago to honour Adhi Buddha, the primordial Buddha. While he's sometimes shown in human form, the Adhi Buddha is closer to the Christian Holy Spirit, an elemental being formed from the collective wisdom of all Buddhas and bodhisattvas (enlightened Buddhist scholars) and not tied to normal planes of existence. }

THE LEGEND OF SWAYAMBHUNATH is tied to the geography of the valley. The Adhi Buddha is said to have manifested as a burning lotus blossom floating on a sacred lake which, when drained by a devout bodhisattva from China, created the Chobhar Gorge. As the waters receded, the lotus was left standing on a small hillock, the site of the temple.

ALSO KNOWN AS the Monkey Temple, Swayambhunath gives a panoramic view over Kathmandu, particularly striking in the evening when the city is lit up. Steep stone steps rise to the base of the stupa, lorded over by Buddha's golden eyes, while wild monkeys swing on the strands of prayer flags.

BUDDHISM IS CLOSER to a philosophy than a religion. By following the eightfold path created by Sakyamuni (the historical Buddha), Buddhists strive to achieve a state of mind that frees them from suffering and the endless cycle of death and reincarnation. Nevertheless, Buddhism still has its rituals, probably the most striking of which is the circumambulation of stupas and Buddhist shrines. Circumambulation is intended to focus the mind on the principle that the pursuit of enlightenment sits at the centre of human life.

REAP
WHAT YOU SOW*

{ *** LIFE FOR KATHMANDU'S ONE MILLION BUDDHISTS AND HINDUS IS DEFINED BY KARMA – THE LAW OF CAUSE AND EFFECT.** According to this ancient philosophy, every action has consequences and repercussions, either in this life or the next. Good deeds can lead to rebirth in higher planes of existence; evil actions reduce humans to the level of unthinking animals in their next incarnation. }

THERE'S A BIG DIFFERENCE between karma and the punishments for breaking moral taboos in Western religions, however. Instead of being a judgment handed down by a god, karma is considered part of the mechanics of the universe – everyone has a choice between using it for self-improvement or suffering the consequences of negative actions. You can see the pursuit of good karma in action all over Kathmandu – in acts of charity, in the huge mounds of offerings at shrines and temples and in the footsteps of the pilgrims at the great stupa at Bodhnath.

30.

HOLY
ROLLING STONES*

{ ***HINDUISM IS ONE OF THE FEW RELIGIONS THAT POSITIVELY ENCOURAGES PEOPLE TO DROP OUT OF SOCIETY.** Every year, hundreds of Nepalis abandon their jobs and all their material possessions to become sadhus – wandering holy men who live off alms and perform extreme acts of self-denial to improve their spiritual wellbeing. The ultimate role model for sadhus is Lord Shiva himself. According to legend, the trident-toting god spent ten thousand years meditating in the Himalaya and smoking charas (hash) to achieve a state of higher spiritual consciousness. Even today, sadhus are the only people in Nepal who are legally permitted to smoke marijuana. }

IN EXCHANGE for donations of money and food, sadhus place a tilak on the forehead of devotees, a symbol of blessing from the gods. The tilak can range from a small dot to a huge smear of coloured powder and rice, and wearing the mark is a sign of divine protection.

33.

ONE OF THE GREAT wellsprings of mystic philosophy is the notion of a universal oneness, embracing all creation. By renouncing materialism for spirituality, sadhus strive to achieve moksha, oneness with the infinite. One device sadhus use to bring themselves closer to god is mala (strings of prayer beads) made from seeds of the holy rudraksh tree. These small, deeply contoured seeds are believed to protect the wearer from impious deeds or thoughts. The surfaces of the seeds are studied intently, as different lines and indentations are believed to respond to different celestial bodies. There is even a busy industry in fake rudraksh mala, with auspicious lines added artificially by human hands.

LIVING GODDESS*

{ *A VAST PANTHEON OF SUPERNATURAL DEITIES ISN'T ENOUGH FOR THE PEOPLE OF KATHMANDU.** The city also has its own living goddess, the Kumari Devi, who resides in an elaborate palace near Durbar Square. Worshipped as an incarnation of Durga, the goddess takes the form of a young girl from the caste of gold and silver-smiths, and is selected from thousands of candidates by a complicated series of astrological and physical tests. }

GIRLS CHOSEN to be the Kumari enter the palace at age four and retire at puberty, triggering a nationwide hunt for the next incarnation of the living goddess. On retirement, Kumaris return to a normal life of school, housework and eventually marriage.

THERE ARE several theories about the origins of the Kumari – according to the most popular one, the Malla king Jayaprakash made inappropriate advances to the guardian goddess of the valley and as punishment, she set him the task of finding her reincarnation among the ordinary families in Nepal.

A BLOODTHIRSTY BUSINESS*

{ *** THE WORD 'PUJA' DESCRIBES A VAST ARRAY OF ACTS OF HINDU WORSHIP, FROM SIMPLE OFFERINGS OF WATER AND FLOWERS** to the gory animal sacrifices generally reserved for more terrifying gods who require a little extra to be appeased. Animal sacrifice has its roots in human sacrifice, but now the victims are goats, buffalo, doves and chickens, sacrificed in their hundreds at temples across the Kathmandu Valley in honour of Lord Shiva and his bloodthirsty consort Durga. }

THE MOST GRUESOME display takes place at Hanuman Dhoka during the October Dasain festival, which celebrates the victory of the goddess Durga over the forces of evil, personified by the buffalo demon Mahisasura. For Hindus, Durga signifies fearful power combined with intense beauty. She's certainly a femme fatale for the goats and buffalo that graze outside temples – they're destined to die at midnight on the eighth day of Dasain, with a single swipe of the sacrificial sword. After further sacrifices the next day, blood is sprinkled on the wheels of vehicles to ensure a safe year on the road.

ENERGETIC*

{ **WITH JUST OVER ONE MILLION PEOPLE, KATHMANDU IS ONE OF THE WORLD'S SMALLER CAPITAL CITIES,** but the incredible crowds on the streets make it feel much bigger. Nowhere is this more obvious than in the old town – a bubbling, bustling melting pot of all the cultures in the Himalaya, with an energy you can almost taste in the air. A walk through the jam-packed alleys near Asan Tole on a busy shopping day is a frenetic, energising experience – or a lesson in agoraphobia, depending on how you deal with crowds. In the old bazaar, saris swirl, gold brocade flashes, market traders holler, motorcycle horns honk, rickshaw bells ring and shoppers do anything they can to forge a path through the streaming mass of humanity. }

THEN SUDDENLY YOU TURN a corner and the crowds are gone. You find yourself standing in a medieval courtyard, alone apart from a flock of pigeons, a statue of Vishnu and one bemused-looking dog.

41.

THE MOBS of shoppers in the old town are one thing, the crowds at Kathmandu's festivals are something else. Tens of thousands of pilgrims cram into the streets and devotees haul giant wooden chariots around the valley to honour the idols of their favourite gods and goddesses. Every night in the bars of Thamel, travellers hold their own mini-festivals to celebrate the start and end of their treks to the foothills of the Himalaya.

STILL, ONE OF THE THINGS that makes Kathmandu manageable is being able to escape when the crowds start to close in. The city is full of quiet alleyways, hidden courtyards and rooftop restaurants where you can look down on the crowds from above and catch your breath.

THE BEST TIME to see the city is during the transition from calm to chaos that takes place every morning, when the empty squares suddenly fill with people, bustle and noise. Some places, of course, are never quiet – the Buddhist stupa at Bodhnath for one, with its thousands of circling pilgrims. The only time the energy dies down is during strikes, when the streets are cleared for political marches and sensible people stay at home away from trouble.

NOT ALL THE ENERGY in Kathmandu is about crowds and noise, though. The city is a beacon for followers of eastern religions and many people come here to develop inner energy on yoga courses and meditation retreats in the valley. Other people just enjoy the thrill of being able to buy anything imaginable in the markets of the old town – the hard sell has to be seen to be believed.

TRADING PLACES*

{ *** THE OLD PART OF KATHMANDU IS ONE CONTINUOUS STREET MARKET, WITH WHOLE DISTRICTS DEDICATED TO INDIVIDUAL TRADES.** Buddhist paraphernalia is sold at Thahiti Tole. Gold and silversmiths make and sell jewellery around Indra Chowk, where other traders sell yak-wool blankets and pashminas made from the underhair of mountain goats. Kel Tole is the district for brassware, kitchen pots and topi (the traditional men's hat), while Asan Tole is surrounded by shops selling incense and spices. }

THANGKA PAINTERS, who produce intricate depictions of Tibetan Buddhist deities on cloth scrolls, cluster around Makhan Tole and Tridevi Marg. Patan is famous for its brass and cast bronze statues, while Bhaktapur is the home of ceramics and wood-carving. One product that is unique to Nepal is Bagh Chal (literally 'Move the Tiger'), the national board game played with brass figures of goats and tigers on a brass grid. One player tries to 'eat' his opponent's goats; the other tries to place goats around the tigers to prevent them moving.

PAPIER-MÂCHÉ MASKS FEATURE
heavily in traditional Hindu dances in
the Kathmandu Valley. The
conclusion of Dasain, for example,
is celebrated with processions and
vivid masked dances, featuring
priests dressed as gods and carrying
wooden swords symbolising the
weapon with which Durga slew the
buffalo demon. The most common
masks are of Ganesh, the beloved
elephant-headed god of good
fortune, sinister Black Bhairab, a
fearsome incarnation of Shiva, and
the Kumari Devi, the living goddess.
Children recreate the legends using
colourful puppets with clay or
papier-mâché heads and multiple
arms clutching tiny weapons.

THE LURE OF THE MOUNTAINS*

*THE TOWERING MOUNTAINS THAT SURROUND KATHMANDU HAVE THEIR OWN UNIQUE ENERGY** – an elemental force that has attracted mountaineers for almost a century. Some, like George Mallory, have perished alone in the snow, but others have had the almost spiritual experience of standing on the roof of the world.

KNOWN in Sanskrit as the 'Abode of Snows', the Himalaya are more than just a mountain range. The peaks are a beacon, summoning climbers and trekkers from across the world to test themselves against one of the most challenging environments on earth.

KATHMANDU has always been the starting point for mountain expeditions. During the 1920s and '30s, the major goal was to summit Mount Everest. Many died before New Zealander Sir Edmund Hillary and Sherpa Tenzing Norgay finally succeeded in 1953 – and the world first heard about the Sherpas, now legendary for their skill, hardiness and loyalty as porters for visiting mountaineers.

MOVERS AND SHAKERS *

{ *** WITHOUT DOUBT, THE HARDEST WORKERS IN KATHMANDU ARE THE PORTERS WHO CARRY GOODS AROUND THE MARKETS OF THE OLD CITY,** hauling huge loads of vegetables and hardware on traditional tumplines – woven straps supported on the forehead – that transfer the weight of the load along the length of the spine. It might sound painful but this is one of the most efficient ways to carry heavy loads; the first humans who crossed the Bering Strait to America used the same technique. Many porters are Sherpas, a tribal people from the high Himalaya who moved to Nepal from Tibet in the 16th century. Generations of mountain life have given Sherpas elevated levels of haemoglobin in their blood, making it easier for them to work at altitude. }

CARS AND MOTORBIKES have taken over most of Kathmandu, but in the narrow alleys of the old city the bicycle-rickshaw still reigns supreme. Most of Kathmandu's rickshaws are driven by hard-bargaining wheeler-dealers with fast legs and even faster tongues. They take no prisoners as they cut through the crowds of shoppers and knots of motorcycles and handcarts.

CHARIOTS OF THE GODS *

THE MOST ATMOSPHERIC CELEBRATIONS are reserved for the Indra Jatra festival in August or September, which marks the end of the monsoon rains. At the height of the festival, the Kumari Devi – the living goddess – is paraded through the Kathmandu Valley in a vast ceremonial chariot pulled by hundreds of devotees.

A SIMILAR CHARIOT, topped by a 20-metre-high crown of freshly cut branches, is hauled through the streets of Patan for the Red Machchhendranath festival which falls in April or May. The chariots in both festivals are effectively temples on wheels and the atmosphere is fevered – in past centuries, devotees would throw themselves under the wheels of the chariots to die in the sight of god.

ALL OF NEPAL'S chariot festivals have their roots in the Jagannath festival at Puri in India, the origin of the modern word 'juggernaut'.

53.

SPIRITUAL HIGHS*

{ *** AS THE SOURCE OF MOST OF THE SACRED RIVERS THAT FLOW INTO INDIA AND THE SPIRITUAL RESIDENCE OF THE HINDU GOD SHIVA,** Nepal has a long-established history of yoga and meditation. Dozens of centres around Kathmandu offer training in hatha and other forms of yoga, and there are schools for Nepali massage, Hindu astrology, Buddhist meditation, Tibetan healing and Indian Ayurvedic medicine. A medieval city surrounded by the world's highest mountains is probably the perfect place to take up a new spiritual pursuit. }

ONE OF THE ADVANTAGES of the vast Hindu pantheon is that there's a god for every occasion. Even toothache has its own patron deity – Vaisya Dev – worshipped at a tiny backstreet shrine near Asan Tole. Over the centuries, pilgrims have nailed thousands of rupee coins to the wooden shrine to pray for relief from the agony of abscesses and rotten teeth.

COSMO POLITAN*

{ ***DESPITE BEING ISOLATED FROM THE OUTSIDE WORLD FOR MORE THAN A CENTURY,** Kathmandu has ended up being one of the most cosmopolitan cities in Asia. Exiles have been taking refuge in this remote mountain valley for centuries. The first wave of Hindu and Buddhist refugees came in the 14th century, fleeing north from the Mughal invasion of India. More recent refugees have come from other directions: south from Tibet and west from Bhutan. }

FROM THE 1960s onwards, the refugees were joined by a new wave of voluntary exiles – hippies fleeing east from the Vietnam War draft and the uptight moral codes of the West. With its laid-back way of life and plentiful supply of marijuana, Kathmandu was the perfect end point for the Asia overland and backpacker trail. Many businesses in Thamel are still owned by overlanders who came here in the 1970s to freak out, and never left.

TODAY, KATHMANDU IS HOME to people from across the subcontinent – Lepchas from Sikkim and Bhutan, Changri and Hor people from Tibet, Nagas from Nagaland, Monpas from Arunachal Pradesh, Sikhs from the Punjab, Muslims from the northern plains. Dozens of tribal languages are spoken on the streets and residents follow a bewildering array of religions, from Hinduism, Buddhism and Islam to tribal shamanism and Bonism, the ancient precursor to Buddhism in Tibet.

SINCE THE 1980s, a big chunk of the foreign influence in the city has come from international aid organisations. Almost every industrialised nation in the world has some kind of development project in Nepal and workers for NGOs form the latest batch of expats to wash up on Kathmandu's doorstep. As well as the bars and restaurants of Thamel catering to them, there's a whole subculture of international schools and European soccer clubs in the affluent suburbs of the city.

THE EVIDENCE of these diverse cultural influences is everywhere in Kathmandu – you'll see it in the modern art hanging on gallery walls and the garage bands fusing Tibetan folk songs with American hard rock. Restaurants serve up every imaginable foodstuff from everywhere in the world and the nightlife is the best you'll find for a thousand kilometres in any direction. Most expats agree that Kathmandu is one of the easiest places in the world to live – prices are modest, the people are delightful, the culture fascinating and the weather balmy, except during the rainy months of the summer monsoon.

MOTHER TONGUES*

{ * KATHMANDU WAS THE HISTORIC MEETING PLACE OF THE INDO-ARYAN PEOPLE OF INDIA AND THE TIBETO-BURMAN PEOPLE OF THE HIMALAYA, and each group brought its own traditions, customs and religious beliefs to the Kathmandu Valley. The result was an incredible ethnic diversity. It is only in the last 50 years that all these diverse groups have come together as a 'nation'. As recently as 1951 there was no unifying national language or currency. **}**

TODAY, more than 100 languages are registered as 'mother tongues' by Kathmandu's census board. Nepali, the national language, is only spoken by 50% of the population and tribal languages like Tharu, Chhetri and Tamang are spoken by more people than English, Hindi or Tibetan. Nepal even has its own indigenous sign language for the deaf, spoken by just a few thousand people in and around Kathmandu. Interestingly, the phenomenally successful Nepali fastfood chain Bakery Cafe only employs deaf waiters, providing a safety net for this traditionally disadvantaged section of society.

61.

THANGKA VERY MUCH*

{ *** KATHMANDU IS FAMOUS FOR ITS ELABORATE THANGKA – VIVIDLY COLOURED CLOTH PAINTINGS SHOWING SCENES FROM THE LIFE OF THE BUDDHA.** Traditionally, thangka featured large Buddhist figures in bold primary colours, but more recently, painters have started producing intricate thangka with hundreds of tiny figures marked out in gold, appealing to foreign tastes. }

NOT ALL NEPALI ART is traditional. Many galleries are now showcasing the city's growing modern art scene. Artists like Dil Bahadur Chitrakar and Chungo Tsering are fusing ancient techniques with modern subjects and sensibilities, producing some surprisingly contemporary work. The current Nepali art scene is a melting pot of local and global influences, some environmental, some political and some religious. While much of the work remains figurative, Nepali painters are gaining an international reputation for abstract works. Art still has the power to shock, even in Kathmandu – a recent painting of a pig in a traditional Nepali cap had letters flooding in to the nation's newspapers.

THE BEST
OF ALL WORLDS*

{ ***SINCE THE 1970s, THE SPRAWLING BACKPACKER NEIGHBOURHOOD OF THAMEL HAS EXPANDED DRAMATICALLY,** leaving the original traveller hang-out, Freak Street, looking empty and forlorn. A crush of craft shops, shoestring hotels, backpacker bars and traveller restaurants, Thamel offers the world in a backstreet – shops sell American trekking gear, French sunglasses, English chocolate, German bread, Bhutanese masks, Tibetan furniture, Nepali paintings, Kashmiri carpets, Indian silks and Chinese flasks. Tea comes in dozens of different configurations – iced tea from America, salted tea from Tibet, green tea from China, oolong tea from Japan – and restaurants serve everything from Japanese teppanyaki to English fried breakfasts and Dutch patatje oorlog (fried potatoes with mayonnaise, ketchup and peanuts). }

AS THE FINAL DESTINATION for the first wave of hippy travellers in the 1960s, Kathmandu also has a strong claim to being the original home of the banana pancake, and this traveller institution is still served up at cafés and restaurants across the city.

65.

SHAHS AND GURKHAS*

{ *** UNTIL 1769, NEPAL WAS A LOOSE AFFILIATION OF FEUDAL KINGDOMS, SOME NO BIGGER THAN A VALLEY,** but the Gurkha king Prithvi Narayan Shah united the rival kingdoms into a single nation, establishing the dynasty that still reigns today. Prithvi Narayan founded his capital at Kathmandu and extended the borders of Nepal into India and Tibet before the British trimmed the country down to its current size. }

THOUGH MANY NEPALIS regard the Shah kings as living incarnations of the god Vishnu, Nepal faced civil war when King Gyanendra seized power from the elected government in response to a rising Maoist insurgency that threatened to topple the monarchy. Gyanendra finally agreed in April 2006 to reinstate parliament, but the future of the Nepali royal family remains up in the air.

DESPITE the waning popularity of the Shahs, the Gurkhas remain highly respected. Gurkha soldiers, famous for their courage under fire, are recruited in their hundreds every year by the British Army.

67.

SPICING IT UP*

{ *** THE CUISINE OF NEPAL HAS BEEN SHAPED BY THE SPICES AND SEASONINGS THAT PASSED ALONG THE MEDIEVAL TRADE ROUTE FROM INDIA TO TIBET.** The salt to season Nepali curries came from the coastal plains of India, while peppercorns and cardamoms were imported from the hills of West Bengal and Assam. Ginger arrived from China and the sugar used to sweeten desserts was trekked in from the palm plantations of Kerala and Tamil Nadu. Probably the most well-travelled ingredient of all is the hot chilli pepper – brought by Portuguese traders from South America through Goa and Macau. }

HINDU NEPALIS are predominantly vegetarian and most meals consist of lentil soup, rice and curried vegetables – the ubiquitous dhal bhaat – spiced up with pickled chillies. However, the meat-eating Newaris have a broad range of spicy carnivorous dishes, using every imaginable part of whichever animal has been slaughtered. Unfortunately for travellers, these dishes are usually reserved for religious feast days and other celebrations.

TIBETAN TREATS*

{ * **ALTHOUGH TIBETANS ACCOUNT FOR LESS THAN 1% OF THE POPULATION, THEY HAVE HAD A HUGE EFFECT ON THE CULTURE OF THE NATION.** Perhaps their most profound influence has been on the food – traditional Tibetan dishes such as momos (steamed or fried meat dumplings) and thupka (noodle soup) appear on menus across the country, and even the popular Nepali beer-snack sukuti (dried meat with chilli and ginger) was brought by yak traders crossing the Himalaya from Tibet. }

IN THE FROZEN FOOTHILLS of the Himalaya, tea is served the Tibetan way with salt and butter, and yak herders warm their bones at night with tongba – hot millet beer, served in bound wooden tankards and sipped through narrow bamboo straws.

THESE CHEAP AND FILLING Tibetan staples now form the backbone of traveller food in the valley. Although Thamel is packed with Tibetan restaurants, the best and most authentic momos are served by the Tibetan exiles at Bodhnath. It's another example of Kathmandu perfection.

70.

VIVID*

*WITH ITS TEMPLES, MONASTERIES, MARKETS AND MONKEYS, KATHMANDU COULD WELL BE THE MOST COLOURFUL CITY IN THE WORLD.** From dawn to dusk, the streets are a living riot of colour – rainbows of saris, temples like treasure troves, vivid flower garlands, markets piled high with mangos and everywhere the red and orange robes of sadhus and Buddhist monks. Few of Kathmandu's photographic shops bother to stock black-and-white film – it just wouldn't do the place justice.

THE BEST TIMES TO CAPTURE the colours of Kathmandu are early in the morning and late in the afternoon, when long shadows stretch across the courtyards and the mountains are lit up by the setting sun. The syrupy afternoon light settles on Bodhnath and Swayambhunath just before sunset, lighting up the gilded faces of the Buddha on top of the stupas. Rainy days only deepen the colours, brilliant details all the more vivid against a grey sky.

COLOUR APPEARS unexpectedly in Kathmandu – the sparkle of a gold tooth in a trader's smile, a glimpse of the mountains between the rooftops, a smear of red on the

73.

{ face of an idol, a wreath of marigolds floating on a rivulet of rainwater. The customs and rituals of Kathmandu's Hindus, Buddhists and Muslims are also incredibly colourful and photogenic. }

TIKKA POWDER makes a massive contribution to the colour of the city – the mystical powder is available in every imaginable hue and most locals keep a supply at home for feast days and special occasions. Probably the most colourful event of the year is Holi, the Festival of Colours, in February or March, when tonnes of tikka powder are tossed around in honour of Lord Vishnu. To celebrate the destruction of the evil demon Holika, followers of Vishnu flood into the streets and throw water and coloured powder over anyone and everyone they come across. Attending the festival without being doused in coloured powder is quite a challenge – clothes end up dyed every colour of the Hindu pantheon.

EVEN IF YOU FAIL to capture the colour of Kathmandu on film, it's easy to bring a piece of the city home with you. The craft and antique shops of Thamel are jammed to the rafters with dangling puppets, grotesque masks, polished brass Buddhas, sparkling gemstones, rainbow shawls, brilliant blankets, psychedelic carpets and intricate thangka paintings in iridescent colours.

PRAYERS ON THE WIND*

{ ***PRAYER FLAGS ARE A DISTINCTIVE SYMBOL OF KATHMANDU.** Hundreds of thousands flutter above the city streets, each printed with mantras and prayers that are carried across the city by the Himalayan winds. The wind is believed to activate the mantras, bestowing protection and blessings on the people who place the flags. }

THE TRADITIONAL COLOURS for prayer flags are blue, white, red, yellow and green, but the flags quickly fade, symbolising the Buddhist belief in the impermanence of existence. At the centre of many flags is an image of the Wind Horse bearing the Three Jewels of Buddhism. At the corners may be images of Garuda (a bird), the dragon, the tiger, and the snow lion – sacred animals representing Buddhist virtues.

BUDDHIST SHOPS in the old bazaar sell prayer flags by the hundreds. The streets of the old town are lined with religious emporiums and there are huge spiritual supermarkets on the edge of Thamel.

77.

ALL
THAT GLITTERS *

{
*DESPITE THE HONKING CARS AND MOTORBIKES, THE ATMOSPHERE IN KATHMANDU IS OVERWHELMINGLY MEDIEVAL,** a result of the ancient Newari buildings that line its streets. This has to be some of the most distinctive architecture in the world. The roofs, idols and doorways of pagoda-roofed temples are covered in shimmering gold or gilded brass, often studded with semi-precious stones. Red-brick shop-houses with ornately carved windows and doors line the winding alleyways of the old bazaar, and each new intersection reveals another cluster of gilded Hindu pagodas and Buddhist shrines.
}

THE HISTORY lying around unattended is staggering – this city could be a living museum. It's been an important trading centre for precious metals and gemstones for centuries and the jewellery shops of Thamel and the old town are a veritable Aladdin's cave of gold, silver and sparkling cut stones, especially appealing to Nepali women who traditionally wear their wealth in jewellery. In Kathmandu, all that glitters probably is gold, or at least gold-plated.

79.

BEHIND THE MASK*

{ * **MASKED DANCERS APPEAR AT MOST KATHMANDU FESTIVALS AND THE MASKS ARE INVARIABLY COLOURFUL AND OUTLANDISH,** depicting beautiful celestial beings or terrifying animal spirits and grimacing demons. During the Indra Jatra celebrations in August or September, hundreds of dancers parade through Durbar Square in brightly painted papier-mâché masks that represent the historical incarnations of Vishnu: Matsya the fish, Kurma the tortoise, Varaha the boar, Narsingha the half-man and half-lion, Vamana the dwarf, Parasurama the warrior, Rama the hero of the *Ramayana*, much-loved Krishna the teacher, and the final future incarnation of Krishna who is destined to destroy the world. Patan holds its own masked dances in September or October for the Dasain festival, with more multicoloured masks of Hindu gods and goddesses. }

PERHAPS the most dramatic masks are reserved for the chaam dances that mark the Buddhist New Year – dancers appear as tigers, snow lions, skeletons, demons and Buddhist deities in eye-wateringly colourful parades at Buddhist monasteries across the Kathmandu Valley.

80.

MAKING YOUR MARK*

{ *** MANY KATHMANDU CITIZENS WEAR A RED TILAK MARK ON THEIR FOREHEADS TO SYMBOLISE THE MYSTIC THIRD EYE** and the need for inner reflection. Among women, the mark takes the form of a bindi, a small dot or a line of red in the parting of the hair, signifying marriage. Tilak marks on men are usually a sign of a visit to a temple or shrine; pilgrims are marked with a paste of red tikka powder, yoghurt and rice as a blessing from the temple priests. }

TIKKA POWDER was traditionally coloured with powdered sandalwood or ground turmeric mixed with lime, but modern chemical dyes have allowed for the creation of all sorts of day-glo colours. At the temple of Pashupatinath, just east of Kathmandu, vendors sell huge pyramids of tikka powder in every imaginable hue for Hindu rituals and festivals. Business is particularly brisk in the run-up to Holi, when vast amounts of the coloured powder are thrown around.

SHAGGY YAK STORY*

{ ***YAKS ARE THE PRINCIPAL DOMESTIC LIVESTOCK OF THE HIMALAYA. THESE RUGGED MOUNTAIN CATTLE** are specially adapted to high altitude conditions, with dense, warm coats and an incredible resistance to cold and fatigue. Growing crops is often impossible in the mountains, so locals rely on their yak herds for milk, cheese and butter as well as wool, which is dyed and woven into colourful blankets. }

FOR CENTURIES, traders from the hills have been coming to Indra Chowk in the heart of old Kathmandu to sell brilliant coloured shawls and blankets made from dyed yak wool, joined more recently by delicate creations of cashmere and pashmina. Though yak-wool shawls are warm and durable, they smell like wet sheep; many locals nevertheless prefer them to the latest modern fleeces and down jackets. There's nothing like drinking butter tea in a mountain teahouse, wrapped in a yak-wool blanket to keep out the crisp, cold Himalayan air. You can take the idea even further with yak-wool sweaters, scarves, socks and even long johns.

A THOUSAND SHADES OF RED *

{ *** IN A CITY ALIVE WITH COLOUR, RED STANDS OUT AS THE DOMINANT HUE OF KATHMANDU.** Red is the colour of the bindi dot on the foreheads of married women and the vermilion tilak mark worn by pilgrims at temples and shrines. It's the colour of the saris worn by Nepali women and the bright robes of novice Buddhist monks. It's the colour of the paste smeared on statues of Hindu gods, the sudden splash of blood from animal sacrifices, the colour of fluttering prayer flags and the offerings of flowers on brass puja trays. It's the colour of the brick temples of the old city and the last light before sunset on the snow-covered mountaintops of the Himalaya.

IN RECENT YEARS red has also become the colour of revolution. Red communist flags are flown by Maoist rebels and political graffiti is daubed in red paint on a spread of walls across the city by communist sympathisers. }

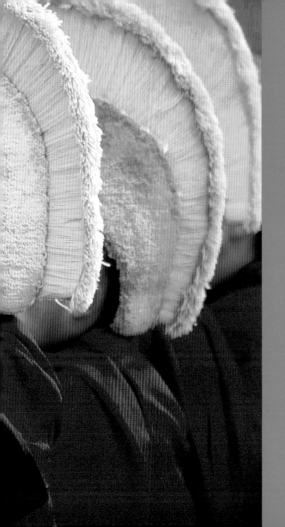

HINDUISM IS THE official religion of Nepal, making it the only officially Hindu nation. However, many of the differences between Hinduism and Buddhism are very subtle. The two faiths share common temples and deities and many of Nepal's Hindus regularly pray at Buddhist temples (and vice versa).

MOST NEPALI BUDDHISTS follow Tibetan Buddhism, but there are various other denominations, linked to the philosophies of individual monasteries in medieval Tibet. Most are identified by their costume colours. A yellow hat with a fringe like a horse's mane is worn in processions by monks of the Sarma denominations, one of which is the Gelukpa sect headed by the Dalai Lama. The monks of the Nyingmapa order wear similar hats in red.

90.

GOLD STAR

KATHMANDU GETS A GOLD STAR
FOR ITS COLOURS. THE STREETS
ARE A LIVING PALETTE,
FROM THE FLASH OF RED TIKKA
POWDER ON A STATUE TO
THE YELLOW SUNBURST OF
MARIGOLD BLOSSOMS IN A
BACKSTREET MARKET.
EVEN ON GREY MONSOON DAYS,
BOLD SWATCHES OF PRIMARY
COLOUR LIGHT UP THE GLOOM.

91.

MY PERFECT DAY

JOE BINDLOSS

{ * With so many things to see in Kathmandu, the only problem is working out where to start. I'd hire a bike or motorcycle the night before then set out early to explore the sights around the Kathmandu Valley, starting at the Monkey Temple at Swayambhunath, with its epic early morning views over the mist-shrouded rooftops of Kathmandu. Next, I'd cut across town to the atmospheric temples and funeral ghats of Pashupatinath, before grabbing a bite of lunch back in the centre on Durbar Marg. From there it's a short ride around the Tundikhel to Durbar Square to explore dozens of mystical medieval temples and admire the extraordinary indulgence of the old royal palace at Hanuman Dhoka – it's like stepping back 300 years. In the afternoon, I'd stroll through the old bazaars at Asan Tole and Indra Chowk and walk to Thamel to stock up on handicrafts and trekking gear and enjoy a slice of apple pie or a quick banana pancake. Before sunset, I'd whistle over to Bodhnath to catch the evening circumambulation of the great stupa, then finish off the day with a steak and a beer at the perennially popular New Orleans Cafe. Kathmandu perfection.

JOE HAS WRITTEN FOR MORE THAN 25 GUIDEBOOKS FOR LONELY PLANET, INCLUDING LONELY PLANET'S *NEPAL.* He's been dropping into Kathmandu ever since he was a student, lured by the mountains and monasteries and the sense of peace, both inner and outer. He still rates Nepal as one of his favourite countries in Asia. Joe first developed an incurable case of wanderlust on family trips through Europe in the old VW Kombi. When not researching guidebooks Joe lives in northeast London with his partner Linda, and a growing collection of Indian musical instruments, Buddhist statues and Tantric chaam masks.

PHOTO CREDITS

CITIESCAPE
KATHMANDU

OCTOBER 2006

PUBLISHED BY LONELY PLANET
PUBLICATIONS PTY LTD
ABN 36 005 607 983
90 Maribyrnong St, Footscray,
Victoria 3011, Australia
www.lonelyplanet.com

Printed through Colorcraft Ltd, Hong Kong.
Printed in China.

PHOTOGRAPHS
Many of the images in this book are available
for licensing from Lonely Planet Images.
www.lonelyplanetimages.com

ISBN 1 74104 939 3

© Lonely Planet 2006
© photographers as indicated 2006

LONELY PLANET OFFICES
AUSTRALIA Locked Bag 1, Footscray, Victoria 3011
Telephone 03 8379 8000 Fax 03 8379 8111
Email talk2us@lonelyplanet.com.au

USA 150 Linden St, Oakland, CA 94607
Telephone 510 893 8555 TOLL FREE 800 275 8555
Fax 510 893 8572 Email info@lonelyplanet.com

UK 72–82 Rosebery Ave, London EC1R 4RW
Telephone 020 7841 9000 Fax 020 7841 9001
Email go@lonelyplanet.co.uk

Publisher ROZ HOPKINS
Commissioning Editor ELLIE COBB
Editors JOCELYN HAREWOOD, VANESSA BATTERSBY
Design MARK ADAMS
Layout Designer INDRA KILFOYLE
Image Researcher PEPI BLUCK
Pre-press Production GERARD WALKER
Project Managers ANNELIES MERTENS, ADAM MCCROW
Publishing Planning Manager JO VRACA
Print Production Manager GRAHAM IMESON